MONMOUTH
MAY, 2016
JOHN DAVIES

Thomas John Barnardo, His Life, Homes & Orphanages

A Short History

Dennis Burnier-Smith

authorHOUSE®

AuthorHouse™ UK Ltd.
500 Avebury Boulevard
Central Milton Keynes, MK9 2BE
www.authorhouse.co.uk
Phone: 08001974150

© 2010 Dennis Burnier-Smith. All rights reserved.

No part of this book may be reproduced, stored in a retrieval system, or transmitted by any means without the written permission of the author.

First published by AuthorHouse   8/26/2010

ISBN: 978-1-4490-9042-5 (sc)

This book is printed on acid-free paper.

FORWARD

Thomas John Barnardo the 19th century Irish philanthropist; friend of the human race and founder of homes, orphanages and ragged schools for destitute children, firstly in the East End of London and later going on to establish homes nationally and to become an international charity, has held a fascination for me ever since I learned that my father, Gus and his half sister; my aunt Louisa were both Barnardo's children; given up by their mother, my grandmother Nellie Sarah Smith, nee Pepper, because they were neglected, unloved and unwanted ragamuffins.

From what can be ascertained, my father rather enjoyed his time at the boy's home; The Boy's Garden City at Woodford Bridge, although, from what I gleaned from him whilst I was growing up, bullying was to be found there much in the manner of the older boys and the fags in: Thomas Hughes' Tom Brown's Schooldays. Apparently, even though it was endemic, much of this bullying went on unbeknownst to the staff.

His Sister, My aunt Louisa was placed in The Village Home for Girl's at Barkingside, Essex on the same date that my father went into the Woodford Bridge Home for boys.

It goes without saying that Barnardo's homes and orphanages, despite the bullying, served to give a great many underprivileged children a basic education and the wherewithal to fend for themselves in a very cruel world with the chance to emigrate to a new life somewhere within the Empire. The basics to become a tradesman were taught and children were put into service in wealthy households, which is what happened to my father, but of that, more later.

Barnardo, with his philanthropic views, was one of the first people to attempt to alleviate the awful poverty of the time. His attempts to help the poor, abandoned and homeless children were way ahead of his times and worked better than any of the previous attempts, of which there had been many.

It was not my intention, when I decided to write this book, to write an all encompassing biography of Thomas John Barnardo, but more a case of giving a brief history of the man, his homes and his orphanages, mainly in the East End of London and those further afield that had links to his first homes. I have also included some vignettes or potted biographies of the people involved with Thomas John Barnardo and the homes, whether directly or indirectly. People like Disraeli, Lord Shaftesbury and many more.

If I had set out to list all the homes and orphanages and the people residing therein, this work would have ended up as no more than a comprehensive list of homes and dates or a name and number crunching exercise. As it is, I hope it gives an insight into the man and his methods and the people that worked close to him, without it becoming a student's text book.

There is also a short chapter on Barnardo's Charity in its modern guise outlining the differences between the days of the Doctor and how it is run today.

Thomas John Barnardo,
His Life, His Orphanages and Homes.
A Short History.

Contents

Forward v

Chapter One Thomas John Barnardo's Early Years in Dublin and London 1

Chapter Two Stepney Causeway The First of Dr Barnardo's Homes And Related Homes 16

Chapter Three Sarah Louise (Syrie) Elmslie 24

Chapter Four The Village Home for Girls, Barkingside, Essex 26

Chapter Five The Death of Thomas John Barnardo 33

Chapter Six Woodford Bridge Boys Garden City & Labour House for Destitute Youths 36

Chapter Seven Watts Naval Training School 45

Chapter Eight Medical Care & The Milne Family at Barnardo's ... 48

Chapter Nine Hints of Controversy and Corruption At Barnardo's Homes 50

Chapter Ten Boarding Out and Emigration From Barnardo's 54

Chapter Eleven Barnardo's Today 59

CHAPTER ONE
THOMAS JOHN BARNARDO'S EARLY YEARS IN DUBLIN AND LONDON

Thomas John Barnardo was born in Dublin on 14th July 1845, the fourth of six children and although his name is synonymous with orphans, orphanages and his ragged schools for destitute children, not a lot is known about Barnardo's early life in both Dublin and in London. Thomas John Barnardo was the son of a Jewish furrier of Spanish or German origin, named John Michaelis Barnardo and Abigail Matilda Barnardo, nee O'Brien who was the daughter of a respected, English, Quaker family. Abigail Matilda's maiden name is sometimes given as Drinkwater; this in actuality was her mother's maiden name. Her mother eloped with an Irish boy by the name of John O'Brien and the product of that union was Abigail Matilda.

*

John Michaelis Barnardo was born in the town of Havelburg, Germany in 1800 and some time after his birth he and his parents settled in Dublin. He married Abigail Matilda O'Brien at the German Church in London on 23rd June 1837 and upon returning to Ireland they took up residence at number 4 Dame Street, Dublin; the house from which John Michaelis ran his furriers business.

*

At his birth, which was a difficult one, Thomas John Barnardo was a small and delicate child and he was not expected to live through the night. His mother, Abigail had also fallen ill due to the difficulties of the birth and she could not nurse her new born child as the doctors recommended and Thomas was put into the care of a wet nurse. The young child rallied and gradually his health and strength improved, but he was to become a cause for concern on further occasions throughout his early years. It is said that at the age of two years a serious illness, most probably diphtheria, was visited upon Thomas John Barnardo and he was pronounced dead by two separate doctors. An undertaker was called but before the funeral director could place the small body in the casket, Thomas was seen to stir, his eyes fluttered and other small movements were noticed; he was not, after all, dead. He was speedily removed to a place of care; his well-being and constitution slowly improved over the ensuing months. He slowly regained his health and strength and grew to become a hardy young man, although shorter than most. He never grew taller than five feet three inches. It seems that the wrongful confirmation of death was probably not as rare as people think it was in Victorian times.

It is probable and more than likely that the lad had a far from happy childhood. He was a slightly built, small individual; probably due, at least in some part to his frailty as a young child, this would have led to him being teased and tormented by his fellow pupils. His early education included St Ann's Sunday school, and at the age of ten he was sent to St John's parochial day school in Fishamble Street, not far from his home on Dame Street. He later followed his two elder brothers, George and Frederick, into the Reverend Dundas' school, better known as St Patrick's Cathedral Grammar School, Dublin; the oldest school in Ireland and ran at the time by the Rev; William Dundas, described by Thomas John Barnardo as a cruel bully of a man who took great delight in beating his pupils for any infringements of his rules.

Young Barnardo was said to have an independent attitude; a free and progressive thinker, he read radical tomes by Jean Jacques Rousseau, the author of 'Emile' and Thomas Paine who wrote 'Rights of Man' and 'Common Sense.' Rousseau actually put his own children into orphanages soon after they were born and Paine is credited with coining the phrase 'The United States of America'.

*

Thomas Paine was the son of a Quaker corset maker and was born at Thetford, Norfolk on 29th January 1737, he was educated at the local grammar School and upon finishing his education he tried various modes of employment. He firstly followed in his father's footsteps and tried corset making in Kent, then as an excise man in Lincolnshire and a schoolteacher in London. While he was employed as a corset maker he met and married Mary Lambert on 17th September1759. The couple moved to Margate where in 1760 Mary died. On March 26th 1771 he married Elizabeth Ollive, the daughter of his landlord, a tobacconist named Samuel Ollive who had died in 1769. Elizabeth and Thomas separated in 1774 but he still sent her money and always spoke well of her. When he moved to London he became acquainted with the American politician, scientist and prolific inventor Benjamin Franklin (17th January 1706 - 17th April 1790) who encouraged him to emigrate to America. Franklin, who was born in Boston, Massachusetts, was in England for discussions with the heirs of William Penn over the future of Pennsylvania; the American Colony was considered their personal property by Penn's heirs. Paine took the advice of Franklin and settled in Pennsylvania where he became a journalist. He published a number of articles in the 'Pennsylvania Magazine,' one advocating the abolition of Slavery. He was a progressive thinker and in 1776 he published 'Common Sense,' a tract that decried the British Monarchy and argued for American independence. He wrote on the superiority of republican democracy over rule by a monarch and travelled to France in 1781 to raise money for the American cause. He returned to Britain in 1787, where, in 1791 he published his most influential and controversial work 'Rights of Man,' in which he attacked hereditary government and suggested a House of Commons where laws could be passed that were favourable to the Majority. The book also recommended old age pensions, family allowances, maternity grants and the abolition of the House of Lords. He was indicted for treason for his views and fled to France. While in France and again because of his views, he was imprisoned for eleven months. Upon his release he returned to America where he died in 1809 in New York City, a drunk and a pauper. He was buried at New Rochelle and ten years after his death, Radical Reformer and political journalist William Cobbett, (1763-1835) had his bones disinterred and brought back to Liverpool, England where they were left until after

Cobbett's death. Thomas Paine's remains came under the care of his son but they were seized by the state, as part of his estate when he was declared bankrupt; it is not now known where the remains lie.

Jean Jacques Rousseau was born in 1712, in Geneva to French Huguenot refugee parents. In 1728 after leaving his job as an apprentice engraver he went to France where he became secretary and companion to Madame Louise de Warens, she was twelve years his senior and was at various times a mother figure, a friend and lover. In 1742 he moved to Paris where he became a close friend of the writer, philosopher and Encyclopaedist, Denis Diderot, who commissioned him to write articles on music for the French Encyclopedie. Then in 1745 whilst working as a music copier he met Therese Lavasseur, an ingenuous and naïve, uneducated lady who worked as a seamstress, with whom he soon started co-habiting. She bore Rousseau five children, all of whom were put into orphanages. It seems that Rousseau and his mistress were ill suited to the bringing up of children and that they could not afford to take care of them. The couple never became officially married but lived together until Rousseau's death. In 1760 he published 'The New Heloise,' probably the most widely read novel of his day and in 1761/62 he published 'Emile' a work which changed the way many people viewed education. In 1762 he also published the 'The Social Contract,' one of the most influential books on political theory ever written. Rousseau lived for a while in England but returned, later, to France where he died, at Ermeonville, near Paris of apoplexy on June 2nd 1778.

*

Young Barnardo, because of his active and inquisitive mind, soon became bored with traditional lessons and was therefore seen as subversive, argumentative and somewhat of a troublemaker at school, although, fortunately, he was blessed with the capability to put forward his arguments with strength and eloquence. Despite the fact that he was, undoubtedly, a very bright and intelligent youth, he failed to pass his public examinations and was apprenticed to a local wine merchant.

Abigail Barnardo, along with Thomas John's brothers, was a member of the Plymouth Brethren to which Thomas converted on May 26th 1862. Prior to his conversion he worked, as stated, as an apprentice to a wine merchant and as a clerk and later briefly preached and gave bible readings, as a member of the YMCA, in the slums of Dublin. He also taught bible classes in the Dublin Ragged School.

The Plymouth Brethren, a non-denominational movement, was founded, in Eire by Edward Cronin, The Reverend John Nelson Derby and Anthony Norris Groves. It seems that the association with Plymouth stems from the fact that, before emigrating to Eire to study at Trinity College, to become a missionary, Norris Groves practised dentistry in Exeter and Plymouth and kept in touch with people from that area. He was invited back to Plymouth in 1830 to preach The Brethren's gospel. He later travelled to Baghdad and then to Russia and India, becoming the first Brethren Missionary.

The Plymouth Brethren, to which Thomas John converted, did not, as the name suggests, originate in Plymouth *per se*. Neither did it spring up in just one place but rather, it began, almost simultaneously in a number of places including continental Europe, Dublin, London and of course Plymouth. Evangelical Protestantism emerged in Britain during the 1730's. The conversion of John Wesley in 1738 is often regarded as the beginning of the Protestant Evangelical movement.

*

John Wesley (1703-1791) was the founder of the Methodist Church. He was born at Epworth, Lincolnshire, the son of Samuel Wesley, the rector of Epworth and his wife Susannah. John Wesley was educated at Charterhouse School in London and then at Christ Church College, Oxford. He was ordained in 1725. In 1735 John Wesley and his brother Charles became missionaries in Georgia, America. Upon returning to England three years later he travelled the country preaching to industrial workers, colliers and agricultural labourers. He was also an author and founded the *Methodist Magazine*. He used the profits and royalties from his writings for charitable works, such as the founding of Kingswood School in Bristol, a city where he lived and preached for a number of years. He was also an anti slavery campaigner and preached about the evils of alcohol and gambling.

The evangelical movement in Ireland sprang up in Dublin in the late 1820's and spread nationally. There are numerous evangelical groups and sub-groups, internationally, of which the Plymouth Brethren is just one. The Brethren's beliefs were those of the New Testament and the emphasis was on meeting in groups solely in the name of The Lord Jesus Christ. They had no Churches and held meetings in each others abodes. The groups and sub-groups involved within the evangelical movement were many and somewhat disparate groups who, largely, did not know each other and had no contact.

*

In his teens and after his conversion to Protestant Evangelicalism the young Barnardo made a deliberate choice to train to become a medical missionary in China for the newly formed China Inland Mission. He studied medicine at the London Hospital at Whitechapel in the East end of London. He first found residence close to the hospital at number 30 Coburn Street, Stepney but after a short while moved to 5 Bromley Street with a Mrs Johnson and later while he was still studying medicine he lodged with the Hudson Taylor family.

*

James Hudson Taylor (21st May1832 – 3rd June 1905), was the founder of the China Inland Mission; he was a Protestant Christian Missionary to China. At the time Barnardo stayed with Hudson Taylor, James Hudson Taylor's wife was Maria Jane Hudson Taylor, nee Dyer.

Taylor was born in Barnsley, Yorkshire, the son of a pharmacist and Methodist lay preacher named James Taylor and his wife Amelia Hudson. At about 17 years of age the young Hudson Taylor turned away from his parents Christian beliefs after reading an evangelical tract and in1849 he committed himself to travelling to China as a missionary. Around about that time he came into contact with a Dr Cronin of Kensington. Cronin was a member of the Plymouth Brethren and it is believed that Taylor learned his faith and the New Testament church and mission principles from his contact with the Brethren.

In the year of 1851 he moved to a poor neighbourhood in Kingston-upon-Hull and became a medical assistant to Dr William Harley. A year later he returned to London and began studying medicine at the London Hospital, later The Royal London Hospital, in preparation for his work in China. Taylor left for China on the 19th September 1853, before completing his medical studies.

It was in 1858, whilst working in China, that he met and married Maria Jane Dyer (1837-1970), the orphaned daughter of the Reverend Samuel Dyer of the London Missionary Society. Hudson met Maria in Ningbo, a city of Zhejiang province, where she lived and worked at a girl's school which was run by missionaries.

Because of ill health Taylor Hudson returned to England in 1860 with his wife and second child, a daughter named Grace. Their first child had died in 1858. Also travelling with them was a young Chinese man, Wang Laijun, who was to help with bible translation back in England. It was upon their return to England that the Taylor Hudson's hosted a young Thomas John Barnardo at their house between the years 1865-1866, as a potential missionary candidate.

In all Hudson Taylor spent 51 years in China where he eventually died. His first wife, Maria, died of cholera around 1870 shortly after the birth of their last child. Taylor re-married; his second wife was Jane Elizabeth Faulding (1843-1904), a fellow missionary since 1866. She died in Switzerland, of cancer, a year before her husband died.

*

The London that greeted Thomas John Barnardo in 1866 was a filthy, disease ridden, overcrowded city, although it was a city of great contrasts. To the West of the city was a place where the rich ladies wore the large hooped skirts and dresses known as crinolines and the gents wore the latest fashions of the day with top hats and spats and whose children received a proper education. Compared to the East End, where there had been a massive influx of people to the newly industrialised capital. The city was struggling to cope with the sudden flood of humanity brought on by the effects of the industrial revolution. Much of the overcrowding was concentrated in the East End where the children were uneducated, malnourished, poorly dressed and dirty and where slums, lack of employment, poverty, disease and crime and prostitution were rife. Gangs of pickpockets went up 'west', to operate where the rich pickings were to be found, They were probably managed or seen over by a gang master and fence much in the guise of Dickens' Fagin, to whom they would return back 'east' with their loot. Down by the River Thames and the docks, "mudlarks" would scavenge in the low water, tidal mud for any "riches" that they could find and hope to sell for a few pence. Smuggling and pilfering was part of everyday life. There were more illegitimate children born in the capital than anywhere else in the world.

It was the London of gas lamps and lamplighters, chimney sweeps and their boys, who would climb up the chimneys of the coal burning fires to sweep and clean them. It was the London of thick smogs, known as pea soupers and also of disease, filth and infestation. Families lived in dire, overcrowded conditions with, in some cases, a family of six or eight people sharing one room. The houses were of the back to back terrace type with narrow streets between them. The streets sometimes had open sewers running down their centres. Rubbish was dumped into the gutters of the thoroughfares and middens and dung piles overrun with rats were commonplace. Numerous families had to share one water pump which soon became infected due to the prevailing conditions and it was this and the lack of a proper sewage system that led to the outbreaks of cholera. Cholera was not the only infectious disease that affected those that were living in such dire conditions; there were also outbreaks of typhus, smallpox and dysentery. Those were the conditions that confronted Dr Barnardo upon his arrival in the East End.

A few months after Barnardo's arrival, an epidemic of cholera swept through the East End reputedly killing over 5,000 people and leaving many families destitute and unable to cope. Thousands of youngsters were orphaned and ended up on the streets, sleeping rough and begging. Others were forced into a life of begging after being maimed in the factories and mills of the day. It was the epidemic of cholera that first drew Barnardo's attention to the homeless and destitute children in England's cities and especially in London.

*

In April 1865 the Crossness Pumping Station built by the Chief Engineer to the Metropolitan Commission for Sewers, Sir Joseph Bazalgette (1819-1891), was officially opened. Prior to this London in general was regularly struck by water borne epidemics of cholera which killed thousands of people. Drinking water was sourced from the Thames which also accepted the city's effluence. Bazalgette's remit was to design a sewage system which would prevent any sewage produced by the city to enter the Thames close to the Metropolis. He saw to it that the flow of foul water from underground waterways and old sewers was intercepted and diverted along new, low level sewers, built behind the embankments on the riverfront and taken to new water treatment works. By 1866 most of London was connected to the sewer network implemented by Bazalgette, The East End, however, was not included in the programme and this was what caused the massive outbreak of cholera in the East End in 1866.

Bazalgette's sewerage system designs had a significant impact upon the health of the populace of London and also on the appearance of the landscape of the metropolis by the building of both the Albert and Victoria embankments and later the Chelsea embankment. These works replaced the filthy, foul and stinking tidal mud of the Thames and turned them into riverside paths and gardens where the populace could stroll in pleasant surroundings.

*

On the 21st of September 1867, Barnardo passed the preliminary examination for Durham University. In September 1868 at the age of twenty three he started at the London Hospital as a full time medical student. It was while he was a student at the Royal London Hospital that Barnardo put his medical studies on hold as he held fund raising meetings, the first of these being in November 1867 which led, with the help and finance of other medical students, to the opening of his own ragged school in Hope Place. Hope Place Ragged School, at Bull Lane, Limehouse, Stepney E14 was where, on the 2nd of March 1868, he rented, at a cost of eight shillings for the ground floor and a further four shillings for the first floor, two floors of the building that he had part acquired and which, at the time, was seen to be an old donkey stables, wherein he set up the schools; one for boys and one for girls. The building was, in fact, an old cottage that had been converted into a Victorian warehouse and had been used, prior to Barnardo's involvement, by a costermonger, to stable his donkeys. This was Barnardo's first ragged School where he started various money raising schemes including a shoe black brigade and a wood chopping team. The school soon became overcrowded, so Thomas Barnardo obtained a second warehouse by the Regent's canal in London's Mile End and it became the largest ragged school in the capital where destitute and homeless children could get a basic education. Those ragged schools were later to be known by the name of The East End Juvenile Missions. The ragged schools and the missions were not residential homes and no children slept or stayed in them overnight. He also established in the East End 'The Band of Hope' meetings for children and it was at these meetings that he discovered the extent of the plight of the homeless children in the city of London. Band of Hope was originally founded in Leeds in 1847 and was a temperance organisation for working class children from the age of six which met on a weekly basis to listen to lectures and partake in social activities. All members swore a pledge of abstinence and had instilled into them the evils of drink.

One of the boys at a ragged school where Thomas J Barnardo was in attendance in 1866; a lad by the name of Jim Jarvis, who later became one of the first children to be taken in at Dr Barnardo's first home at Stepney Causeway, took Thomas Barnardo around the streets, slums and hovels of the East End to show him where children were sleeping rough on roofs and in roof gutters, in the East End Marketplaces or anywhere where they could find a warm and dry haven. This excursion around the slums so moved Barnardo that he decided to devote his life to helping and alleviating the poverty of those destitute children and thus abandoned the idea of missionary work in China.

Night and Day, the official magazine of Barnardo's homes, which was first published in 1875, carried in one of its issues the following passage in which Barnardo described how he met Jim Jarvis:-

*

One evening the attendants at the ragged school were leaving to go to their places of residence. A little lad who had been listening attentively was one of the last to make his way to the exit. He shuffled hesitantly and unwillingly. Upon noticing the boy Barnardo said 'Come, my lad, had you not better get home? It's very late. Mother will be coming for you.'

The lad answered 'Please sir, let me stop! Please let me stay. I shan't do any harm.'

'Your mother will wonder what has kept you so late.' Barnardo told him.

'I ain't got no mother.' The lad replied.

Haven't got a mother, boy? Where do you live?'

'Don't live nowhere.'

'Well, where did you sleep last night?'

'Down in Whitechapel, sir, along the Haymarket in one of them carts as is filled with hay; and I met a chap and he telled me to come here to this school, as perhaps you'd let me stay near the fire all night.'

*

This meeting further awakened the humanitarian and altruistic attitudes that dominated Barnardo's thoughts and actions and decided him in which way his life should proceed and he committed himself to composing and writing a letter to the Prime Minister of the day, Benjamin Disraeli. That letter written from 26 Chapel Lane, Stepney was to inform the PM about the living conditions of children in the East End. Children that were parentless, had no good water, food or shelter and that had turned to thievery because of their situation. Barnardo then related in the letter his meeting with Jim Jarvis and his tour around the slums of the Whitechapel area. He ended the letter by asking the Prime Minister for money towards his homes for those poor and destitute children.

*

Benjamin Disraeli (1804-1881), was born, at Bedford Row, London, to Jewish parents on the 21st January 1821, but although he was of Jewish descent he was baptised in St Andrew's Anglican Church in 1817. He was educated at Higham Hall School in Walthamstow from 1817-1824 and was later admitted to Lincoln's Inn to study law. He travelled in Europe and the near east as a young man and whilst travelling he contracted Gonorrhoea. In 1925 he founded a local daily newspaper, 'The Representative' which only ran for a few months. His first novel was published in 1826, it was called Vivien Gray and earned him £200. He allied himself to the conservative party of the day after having failed as an Independent Radical in Wycombe. He also continued his career as an author succeeding in having a number of works published; 'The Voyage of Captain Popanilla' in 1828 and 'The Young Duke' in 1831, amongst others. In August 1939, he married Mary Anne Wyndham

Lewis, twelve years his senior and the widow of his friend and fellow politician Wyndham Lewis. The union was childless probably due to the gonorrhoea that Disraeli contracted earlier, or perhaps, because she was twelve years his senior, being forty seven years old when they married she was probably past her child bearing days.

In 1841 Robert Peel became Prime Minister and Disraeli became a Member of Parliament for Shrewsbury. Disraeli wrote to Peel asking for a position in his government but was turned down for a government post. He opposed Peel's repeal of the Corn Laws and when Lord John Russell who succeeded Peel, resigned in 1852 the Earl of Derby formed his first administration Disraeli became Chancellor of the Exchequer. He had a turbulent political career, crossing swords with Peel, Gladstone and others. He, again, became Chancellor of the Exchequer under the second ministry of Earl Derby in 1858 and again in 1866. Disraeli became Prime Minister on the resignation of Derby. Queen Victoria created Mary Anne Disraeli the Countess of Beaconsfield; she died in 1872 leaving Disraeli distraught. In the 1874 General Election the Conservatives won and Disraeli formed his second ministry and in 1878 he was raised to the House of Lords as the Earl of Beaconsfield. In 1880 he resigned as Prime Minister after a Liberal victory; he then became leader of the opposition from the Lords. Disraeli died the next year; he was seventy six years old.

*

Barnardo was a powerful and voluble orator and at the Missionary Conference held at the Agricultural Hall, Islington in 1867 he made a rousing and moving speech about the destitute and homeless children and the problems that they faced. In the audience was Anthony Ashley Cooper, 7th Earl of Shaftesbury (1801-1885), who, like Barnardo was a philanthropist. The Victorian era was seen as the golden age of philanthropy. He was, for 39 years, the holder of the Office of Chairman of the Ragged Schools Union. Shaftesbury Avenue was named after Earl and it was opened a year after his death and although its route took in streets that were already in existence, its construction and formation brought about the demolition of a great many of the appalling slums that he had sought to eliminate in his lifetime. During his life he was involved in factory reform and was responsible for seeing three Factory

Acts through Parliament. He was also involved with the Coal Mines Act of 1842 which was instrumental in ending the employment of women and children less than thirteen years of age, working below ground in the mines. Shaftesbury was one of the founders of The Ragged Schools Union which had far reaching effects throughout the United Kingdom. In the early days of the ragged schools, any buildings that could be utilised were used as classrooms including stables, lofts and railway arches. As the schools developed many gained better premises and served a wider clientele with a broader curriculum. The Earl was so moved by Barnardo's oration that he offered Barnardo help to establish homes for the homeless and destitute children.

Robert Barclay (1843-1913) of the Barclay's banking family, who was responsible for the merger of twenty banks in 1896 forming the Barclay and Company Limited Bank, which changed its name to Barclay's Bank Limited in 1917, also agreed to support the cause along with Hugh McCalmont the First Earl Cairns (1815-1885)]. McCalmont was born in Belfast and educated at Trinity College, he became a lawyer in 1844 and a Member of Parliament for Belfast from 1852 to 1866 he was raised to the peerage in 1867, he held office as Solicitor-General in1858, Attorney-General in 1866, Lord Chancellor in Disraeli's administration and again in Disraeli's 2nd administration of 1874-1880. Throughout Gladstone's administration of 1868-1874 Cairns was leader of the opposition in the House of Lords.

A £1000 donation was received from MP Samuel Smith to further enhance the money which had become available for the first home for destitute children.

Because of the support and patronage of these very prominent and famous people, enough money was raised by the 2nd March 1868, to open the first home, although, because of the logistics of the task, this first home did not open until 1870.

In those early years Thomas John was known as Dr Barnardo although he had no legal right to use title of doctor as he had taken time out from his medical studies in pursuance of his benevolent and philanthropic work of rescuing destitute children. The title, therefore, was an honorary one.

*

Ragged Schools were nothing new in Barnardo's Time. He had, himself, taught and given bible readings in the Dublin Ragged School as a young man, before coming to London. The idea of the ragged school was developed by John Pounds (1766-1839), a Portsmouth shoemaker. Pounds was the son of a dockyards sawyer who managed to secure his son a position as an apprentice shipwright, unfortunately, the younger Pounds fell into a dry dock and was crippled. Unable, after the accident, to carry on his apprenticeship or work as a shipwright he learnt shoe-making and in 1803 started his own business. It was whilst working in his shop that he started to teach the poor, working class children to read. His reputation as a teacher spread and besides reading and arithmetic he started to teach carpentry, cooking and shoemaking. Unlike other schools of the time John Pounds did not charge a fee for teaching the poor of Portsmouth. Free education for orphans and those that were destitute and unable to pay became the principle upon which the ragged schools operated.

In the same mould as John Pounds was Thomas Cranfield; a tailor and former soldier. He opened a Sunday school, offering free education, on Kingsland Road, London. Kingsland Road now forms part of the A10 Cambridge Road. In 1798 he established a day school on Kent Street close to London Bridge. By the time of his death, in 1838, he had built up an organisation of nineteen schools in the poorest and foulest parts of London; they were comprised of Sunday schools, night schools and day schools.

The ragged school movement in Scotland actually started in 1841when Sheriff Watson, upon seeing the number of poor, homeless juveniles coming before him in his courtroom accused of petty crimes, resolved, rather than sending them to prison, to establish a school for the youths. In 1841 he opened his Industrial Feeding School where the three 'R's were taught and besides being given three meals a day the boys could learn a trade such as printing or shoemaking. A girl's school followed in 1843 and a mixed school was founded in 1845.

The Reverend Thomas Guthrie (1803-1873), preacher and philan-thropist and founder of the Free Church of Scotland, helped to promote the idea of free teaching of the poor, working class children. He saw the link between poverty and ignorance and founded a number of ragged schools in the Edinburgh area. He was an abstainer from strong drink and a firm opponent of alcohol abuse and he realised that a lot of abused children came from homes where alcohol was also abused.

In 1844 the movement spread to England when Lord Shaftesbury formed the Ragged Schools Union and by 1852 two hundred free schools were established for poor, working class children throughout Britain. The wealthy, philanthropic individuals such as Angela Bartlett-Coutts, (1814-1906), the granddaughter of the banker, Thomas Coutts, whose wealth she inherited, donated large sums of money to the Ragged Schools Union. Those donations helped to establish three hundred and fifty ragged schools by the time the 1870 Education Act was passed, after which the number of pupils at the ragged schools declined.

The 1870 Education Act, or the Forster Act, named after its author W.E. Forster, and which set in motion the division of the country into two thousand five hundred school districts and stated that school boards were to be elected by ratepayers in each district. Local ratepayers were asked to build a primary school in any area where one did not already exist. The local school boards had the right to compel children to attend these primary schools at a nominal fee. By 1874 over five thousand new schools had been founded but it was not until 1891 that education was supplied free. Although it had been compulsory up to the age of ten since 1880; (it was raised to age of twelve in 1899), education in Great Britain was still well behind countries such as France and Germany. However, until 1900, schooling was only up to primary level and it really wasn't until the 1902 and another Education Act known as the Balfour Act that things improved by the provision of funding for secondary education out of local rates with grants made available from Central Government. In 1907, a scholarship scheme was introduced which allowed the cleverer youngsters from poorer backgrounds to go to secondary schools. There were further improvements and by 1914 a well organised system of education was in place.

*

CHAPTER TWO
STEPNEY CAUSEWAY
THE FIRST OF DR BARNARDO'S HOMES
AND RELATED HOMES

Number 18, Stepney Causeway was the first of Dr Barnardo's homes to be opened in December 1870 on a ninety nine year lease at fifty seven pounds per annum. It was cited as a home for working and homeless boys. Over the years the home was extended and it grew as further properties were obtained. From 1908 it provided training for a trade and general education for those that resided there. The original home at number 18 Stepney Causeway closed around 1922/23 but other buildings along the Causeway had been obtained earlier on as the need for more facilities grew and the work to save those in poverty continued unabated.

Number 10 the Causeway was an open all night centre which was opened in 1874 for homeless children. Number 19 on Stepney Causeway opened in 1877 as a hospital unit for sick children and number, 1 Bower Street adjacent to the Causeway opened in 1885 as a half way house for boys. In 1908 it was used for boys with suspected infectious diseases.

Boys Garden City, Woodford Bridge

Stepney Causeway, London

By 1888, after numerous additions, it was said that the huge dining room was bright and airy, lined with glazed tiles throughout and that the kitchens included a large bakery where some of the lads were trained as cooks and bakers. There were extensive bathrooms and toilets and a large swimming bath. There were also workshops where the lads were taught carpentry, engineering, brush-making, shoe-making and tailoring.

Numbers 12, 13 and 16 Stepney Causeway were opened in 1899 as the Marie Hilton crèche day nursery for babies and young children of working mothers. The Causeway home was further extended taking in numbers 21, 23, 25, and 27. Number 30 opened in 1903 and was used for children with infectious diseases until it closed around 1914. In 1940 Stepney Causeway in its modern guise closed for the duration of the war, except for number 4, which opened in 1941, as a temporary boy's hostel for those over fourteen years of age. It closed in April 1967.

Not long after the opening of his first home for homeless and destitute boys at number 18 Stepney Causeway in the East End of London a youngster; an Eleven years old boy named John Somers and nicknamed Carrots, called at the home seeking shelter. Unfortunately, the home, on that night, in 1871, was full and young Somers was turned away. Two days later he was found dead from malnutrition and exposure. From that time forth the home bore a sign proclaiming 'No Destitute Child Ever Refused Admission.' Thomas John Barnardo actively went out each night into the slum districts of the East End to seek out and find destitute children.

It was after the death of John Somers that Dr Barnardo in 1874, opened the first of his 'Ever Open Door' homes at number ten Stepney Causeway. As the name suggests it was open all night. No child was ever turned away and a bath, a comfortable bed and breakfast were always ready for the waifs and strays. The next morning the child was turned over to the Home a few doors away where they would be looked after and cared for. The number of homeless children in the East End dictated that number ten soon became regularly full and so numbers 6 and 8 were added to the Ever Open Door Centre.

The well to do and better off people of London at the time viewed poverty as shameful and a result of laziness and vice. Those same people saw nothing wrong in sending children up chimneys or working children as young as seven years old in the mills and factories for up to fourteen hours a day in filthy and dangerous conditions. Injuries within the workplace were common and those that were badly injured in pursuance of their employment and could no longer work were cast out without any recompense. The owners of these work establishments saw hard toil as the saviour of the poor people's souls, not to mention the vast riches they made out of their exploitation of minors.

During the Victorian era and while William Wilberforce (1759-1833), Member of Parliament for Hull and abolitionist was doing his great work to abolish the negro slave trade to the British Colonies, back home in England young children of both sexes were being treated little better than slaves; fodder for the industrial revolution and a means of maximising profits for the magnates and captains of industry who cared little for the welfare and health and safety of the poor children that they employed under dire conditions or for that matter for the adults who were also paid very little for their labour and who also had to work long hours under filthy and dangerous conditions.

During 1874 Barnardo opened a photographic department in the Stepney boys' home and over the following years, every child that was taken in by Barnardo's had his or her photograph taken there. The taking of those before an after photographs continued at least until the time that my own father and his half sister were taken in by Barnardo's Homes in August 1930. *(See photographs on Pages 41 & 44)*. The children were first photographed when they were initially admitted to the home and then again, a few months after they had been cared for and they had recovered from their ordeals and experiences of living rough on the streets. The difference between the earlier photographs and those taken later were markedly pronounced. In the later photographs the children looked healthier and were cleaner and better nourished, they had neat haircuts and better clothing, their health and well being had improved immensely. Their whole appearance had changed for the better; they had smiles upon their countenances where before, their faces bore scowls and grimaces and showed nothing but abject fear.

Barnardo was an entrepreneur; a master at spotting opportunities to raise cash for his charitable foundations and to allow him to build up funds for the running of the orphanages and to publicize his work and raise money for his charitable work. Besides selling religious tracts Barnardo sold these 'before and after' picture cards in packs of 20 for 5 shillings, (25p), or singly for 6 pence, (2 ½p).

Stepney Causeway closed as a home for the homeless and destitute on the 19th April 1922 when two hundred and sixty boys marched out of Stepney to their new home, The William Baker Technical School at Goldings, Hertford in Hertfordshire. The Causeway closed its doors as the Charity Headquarters, for the last time in 1969 when the staff moved to their new Headquarters at Barnardo House, Barkingside, next to the Girl's Village Home.

The building which became The William Baker Memorial Technical School for boys was purchased on 19th April 1921. It was refurbished and made ready for the boys of Stepney Causeway. The school should have opened on the 15th November but, unfortunately, a General Election had been called for on that day and so, the then Prince of Wales, officially opened the school two days later on 17th November 1922. The technical School closed in July 1967, although the printing department remained open until the official opening of Barnardo's School of Printing in Mead Lane, Hertford in 1969. The school never served as a home, it was built in 1968 at the cost of £40,000 and opened in September 1969 to serve those boys left at the old printing department. Because of the expense of running the apprenticeships plus general running costs it was deemed to expensive to continue and Barnardo's closed the School of Printing in March 1991.

Another of the homes that had connections with Stepney Causeway was Leopold House situated at 199 Burdett Road, Stepney, East London; it was named after the youngest son of Queen Victoria, Prince Leopold, Duke of Albany and was opened in 1883 for orphaned boys between the ages of ten and fourteen when, upon attaining that age, they would be moved to Stepney Causeway. During 1886 and 1887 Leopold House was altered and extended with a new house being built to the rear of the old building. Upstairs the new house contained a two hundred bed dormitory, apartments for masters and matrons. Downstairs was a dining hall capable of seating four hundred and fifty, there was a large plunge bath and a capacious swimming pool with changing rooms.

The old house contained the large, well equipped kitchen in which food for the whole household was prepared and served. Also in the old building were six small dormitories, offices, and a playroom and outside was a large playground. Leopold House closed in 1912 on the opening of larger accommodation at Stepney Causeway. The superintendent of Leopold House, a Mr Armitage, moved, with the rest of the boys to Dame Margaret's Home at Washington, County Durham. When Barnardo's vacated Leopold House the building was taken over by the Salvation Army for use by the homeless of the area. Permission for the designated usage was refused by Stepney Borough Council in 1915 after a protracted dispute and Leopold House was eventually given over to a shoemaking factory. During the Second World War, Leopold House was finally destroyed when it suffered a direct hit by a German bomb in 1941.

Dame Margaret's Home, Washington, County Durham was opened as a Barnardo's Home in1889 as a home for boys and girls aged between five and fourteen years. The home was named for the wife of Sir Isaac Bell, founder of the Washington Chemical Works and one time Lord Mayor of Newcastle upon Tyne. After the death of his wife, Margaret, in 1871, Sir Isaac gave Washington Hall to be used as an orphanage and it was renamed Dame Margaret's Home, it was purchased outright by Barnardo's in 1910.

Mr Armitage, who had come from Leopold House, upon its closure, was responsible for the welfare of the boys while his sister Miss Armitage looked after the girls. There were no educational facilities at the home and the children were marched the half mile to the local school for their educational needs. From 1939 and throughout the war Dame Margaret's Home was used as an evacuation home and was finally closed in 1946 with the children moving to Beaconsfield House, at Cullercoats, North Shields which was opened in 1946 and was situated on the seafront at Cullercoats, it finally closed as a Barnardo's Home in September 1953.

From the initiation of the first home the work for the needy and the homeless children increased steadily until, at the time of his death in 1905, there were established one hundred and twelve district homes besides mission branches throughout the United Kingdom. The reason for which these homes were established was to search for and to receive waifs and strays; to feed, clothe and educate and where possible provide them with industrial training. The fundamental basis for Barnardo's homes was that of free and immediate admission, with no restrictions concerning age, sex, religion or nationality. The only fixed requirement was that of destitution.

Barnardo was a teetotaller and was active in the Temperance Society and after his first home was up and running he managed to buy a notorious pub, music hall and gin palace called the Edinburgh Castle in Rhodeswell Road, London. His plan was to shut down what he saw as a den of iniquity where children could be corrupted. His plan then, was to refurbish it and convert it into 'The Coffee Palace and Mission Hall' where children could be guided along the path of righteousness. After much renovation and refurbishment at a great cost it was officially opened by Lord Shaftesbury in 1873. It was used as a meeting place where the good word was preached and it became a significant centre for evangelism until 1927 when Barnardo's ceased to have any connection with The Edinburgh Castle. It was finally demolished in 1952 to make way for the Mile End Stadium, although the multi sports complex never actually opened on that site until 1990.

The Doctor also sold religious pamphlets in London's public houses to help raise funds for his charitable works. This sometimes led to him being attacked, for his efforts, by the rather rough and somewhat irreligious clientele. These attacks sometimes led to injuries, one such attack resulting in him sustaining two broken ribs. A chapter from *Night and Day*, the official Dr Barnard's Homes Magazine, describes such an attack in what may be construed as comic terms:-

*

'I entered the door. At first I could hardly see who were the occupants. It was a long, narrow room, with a bench running all around it on which sat lads and girls aged between 14 and 18 years; the view was obscured by a cloud of tobacco smoke that completely filled the room.

Advancing into the centre of the room I declared that I had come to sell the word of the God and announced that I would give the whole bible for thre'pence, The New Testament for a penny.'

'Chuck him out.' cried one of the customers.

'For the most part all in the room were under the influence of drink, and although many of them were girls and boys they were wild and beyond control. I presently found myself on the ground with the flat part of a table pressing upon me. Its legs being in the air, whilst several of the biggest lads leapt inside it, dancing a 'Devil's Tattoo, to my great discomfort.'

*

Part of the Stepney Causeway complex was John Benn House, at 1 Bower Street which was opened in 1885 and later purchased in1889. John Benn (1850-1922) whom the house was named after was born in Hyde, Manchester and moved to London with his family. He became a member of the London County Council and he backed the London dock strike in 1889. He was involved in charitable work in and around London. The premises were sold to East End Hostels Association in January 1927. It was repurchased by the Dr Barnardo's Homes, after the Second World War in 1949. The premises were kept by Barnardo's until the whole Stepney Causeway complex closed in 1972.

It was in the Doctor's lifetime that eleven small houses in Bower Street came onto the market. These houses, due to their proximity to John Benn House and Stepney Causeway, had long been desired by the Doctor to become part of the Stepney Causeway complex. Within a year those much sought after additions were in regular use. The playground, which was deemed too small, was extended, as was the drill yard where the boys took morning exercise. The new buildings were connected to those in the Causeway by a covered bridge.

Because it was seen as advantageous to teach the boys a method whereby they could earn a living, there was a trade block attached to the rear of the main building where many and diverse trades could be learned, these included shoe making, brush making, carpentry, tailoring and engineering. There were also workshops for blacksmiths, tinsmiths, wheelwrights, printers and for harness and mat making.

CHAPTER THREE
SARAH LOUISE (SYRIE) ELMSLIE

Sarah Louise Elmslie was born in1847; known as Syrie she was the daughter of William Elmslie and Betsy Sarah Elmslie nee Mumford of Kings Bench, Middlesex. William Elmslie was at that time the Chairman of Lloyds. Syrie met Barnardo when she contacted him to persuade him to give a speech at a meeting in Richmond, Surrey. Syrie shared Barnardo's views and passion for philanthropy and evangelicalism. The meeting proved to be fortuitous for Barnardo for on the 17th June 1873 when she was 25 years of age and Barnardo was 27, the couple were married. They spent their honeymoon at Lowestoft, staying there for 6 weeks.

As a wedding present the couple were given a fifteen year lease on Mossford Lodge at Barkingside by one John Sands who, at that time, was the chairman of the London Stock Exchange.

The Barnardo's had 6 children between them, 3 of whom died young; another, Marjorie, suffered from Down's syndrome which inspired and influenced Barnardo in setting up homes for children with physical and learning difficulties. Gwendoline Maud Syrie, another daughter of the Barnardo's married Sir Henry Wellcome in 1901; a man 26 years her senior with whom she had one child also called Henry. She had an affair with the author Somerset Maugham to whom she bore a child in 1915. That child was Elizabeth Mary Maugham. Maugham was mentioned in the divorce proceedings and once the divorce was finalised in 1916 she married Maugham in 1917. She divorced Maugham in1929.

Gwendoline Maud Syrie Maugham went on to become a successful interior designer. She died in 1955.

The other Barnardo children were first born, William Stuart E. Barnardo born 1874, secondly Herbert Frederick E. Barnardo born1876 died 1886 of diphtheria, thirdly Kenward Arthur E. Barnardo born 1878 died 12th January 1890, fourth was Gwendoline Maud born 1879 died 25th October 1955, fifth was Cyril Gordon Barnardo born1887, and last born was Marjorie Elaine Barnardo born in1894; she suffered Down's syndrome.

Sarah Louise Barnardo Elmslie passed away on the 21st November 1944 at the age of 97 years.

CHAPTER FOUR
THE VILLAGE HOME FOR GIRLS, BARKINGSIDE, ESSEX

Thomas Barnardo had been refused permission by the Charity Commission, in 1871, to open a girl's home, because of the Victorian standards which stated that he had to have a wife in order to run a girl's establishment. He realised that although there were not as many homeless and destitute girls as there were boys, their destitution often took on a darker aspect than that of the boys; child prostitution was rife at the time and young girls would often be sold to the highest bidder. The age of consent at the time was just 13 years of age. Barnardo decided that something must be done for these highly vulnerable but street wise girls.

*

W.T. Stead was the man instrumental if not responsible for getting the age of consent raised from 13 to 16 years of age. Stead was a newspaper editor who, in 1885, published four articles on prostitution in London entitled "The Maiden Tribute of Modern Babylon." Those four articles had a deep and profound influence on the country as a whole and brought about the introduction of the Criminal Law Amendment Act which finally raised the age of consent to sixteen years.

Stead's investigative methods, however, left him open to prosecution and he served three months in gaol.

Stead, like Barnardo, received support from Lord Shaftesbury. He later became a staunch opponent of the Boer War. His colourful life came to an end on the 14th of April 1912 when, with a host of other unfortunate souls, the Titanic, on which he was a passenger, was struck by an iceberg and he lost his life in the icy waters.

*

After Barnardo had married Syrie and taken up the lease on Mossford Lodge they went to live there. Next to the lodge was a coach house which They decided would be converted into living quarters and in October1873 it was opened up to destitute girls and upon its official opening that year it had places for 12 girls, which soon rose to 54 and necessitated the need for newer and bigger premises.

Barnardo and Syrie continued to live at Mossford Lodge for a while but then moved to a larger house, The Cedars, in Hackney, a gift from Syrie's Father. It seems the reason for this was that Mr Elmslie had concerns about the surroundings that his grand children would be brought up in. It seems, therefore, that even in the midst of the philanthropic work being carried out by his daughter and her husband, snobbery existed. The couple later moved to another property in Surbiton.

By 1875 Barnardo's ambitious plan to create a village home for girls to accommodate over 1000 girls and to replace Mossford Hall was realised. The Girl's Village Home was devised and paid for out of private donations. The donations raised were by virtue of Barnardo's Entrepreneurial endeavours and his knack for making money; selling bibles and religious pamphlets, the before and after photographs etc. As the name suggests, each cottage that was constructed had its own garden back and front and each cottage had a house mother. The foundation stone for Myrtle Cottage was laid by the Rt Hon Earl of Aberdeen on the 9th June 1875 and was named in memory of Mr and Mrs Zaneous Dawson's daughter.

Barnardo had met Mr Dawson on a trip to Oxford, he (Dawson) had had lost his young daughter a few months prior to their meeting. Dawson was resolved to honour his daughter in some lasting way, that way being by the funding of the first cottage to commemorate his daughter. Foundation stones were laid for 13 more cottages and building commenced.

By the 9th July1876 the cottages Myrtle, Woodbine, Clapham, Honeysuckle, Jasmine, Cambridge, Lily, Hawthorn, Daisy, Billiter, Rose, Bluebell, primrose, and Forget-me-not were officially opened by Lord Cairns who arrived barely in time for the opening which was set for 3:30pm. Each cottage cost in the region of £500.00 to build and furnish and housed between 12 and 20 girls.

On the 19thJuly in 1876 the Village Governors house and a new modern steam laundry were completed and opened. The first governors of the Girls Village Home were Dr Henry Solcau and his wife Georges Solcau.

It was also in the year of 1876 that Barnardo left the administration and running of the homes to his trusted staff and resumed his medical studies; he spent around 4 months studying at the Royal College of Surgeons, Edinburgh enabling him to pass his diploma and to qualify as a licentiate of the college, he also became an accredited male midwife. Upon his return to London, in April of that year, he registered as a medical practitioner and could, therefore, use the title of Doctor quite legitimately. Three years later on 16th April 1879 he was elected a Fellow of the Royal College of Surgeons, Edinburgh.

In that same year of 1876, Thomas Barnardo set up a council of trustees to be responsible for charitable donations and any other monies and to be responsible for policy making. These moves enabled him to devolve responsibility to others and leave him relatively free for fund raising and other necessary tasks.

The girls in the Village were trained for going into service in private houses. When they reached the age of thirteen they were placed in one of four divisions. The first division girls were given a uniform to the value of five pounds to wear. That uniform became the girl's own property after twelve months. The girls in the second division were given a uniform to the value of three pounds ten shillings and those in the third division received a uniform to the value of three pounds. The second and third division girls had to pay for their uniforms by way of deductions from their earnings. The girls in the fourth division were those that had been found to be dishonest and who had a penchant for violence and low standards of personal health and hygiene; they would not be sent out to service and they did not receive a uniform. If their behaviour and demeanour did not improve they could be dismissed from the Village in disgrace and sent to a School of Discipline.

Expansion at The Girls Village Home continued with more cottages being opened on the 10th July1878, these were Craven, Salem, Trefoil, Heartsease, and Wild Thyme. They were officially opened by Her Grace Sydney, Dowager Duchess of Manchester.

At the same time cottages Violet, Bath, Halifax, Armitie, Babies, Hahnemann were officially opened by The Countess Cairns. Just under a year later on 18th June 1879, cottages Hyacinth, Eton, and Beehive were opened by HRH. Princess Mary Adelaide, Duchess of Teck.

In 1879 as the village grew Thomas Barnardo advertised for more ladies to become house mothers. These ladies had to be of a religious persuasion, be total abstainers from alcohol and be of a high moral and ethical standard. In the same year an epidemic of Scarlet fever broke out; 150 girls were infected but no deaths were recorded. This speaks volumes about the care and protection that those girls received, for if this outbreak had have happened outside the confines of the village and in the East End area around Stepney or Whitechapel, there would have been a high mortality rate.

In 1880, three more cottages were built and opened. These were May, Clarellan and Heather. The Girl's Village Home continued to grow and by the 6th of August 1887 more cottages had been completed and were opened these last cottages were named: Burwell Park, Curling, Mickleham, Sweetbriar, Pink Clover, Ivy, Oxford, St. Helena, Syndal, Pussy, Joicey, Clement, Mayflower, Cyril, Sir James Tyler, Ilex, Hope and Peace. Alongside these buildings was erected Cairn's House in memory of Hugh McCalmont, Dr Barnardo's first president, Earl of Cairns.

Sometime in the 1880's Dr Barnardo invited some old girls to visit their old home at the Girl's Village Home; he called that first meeting Foundation Day, which year by year became established as a little formal function and even old boys from the Boy's Garden City were invited. The boys, like the girls would renew acquaintances with their old masters and mistresses. The boys would have a game of cricket against their old masters. Foundation Day became a fund raising occasion, with the old boys and girls that were then employed and earning a living, after shaking the Doctor's hand, would leave a small donation to be added to the funds raised elsewhere. Those donations became known as love gifts. Each year the celebrations of Foundation Day came to be held on or close to Doctor Barnardo's Birthday in July.

The Village home continued to expand and in September 1896, Mossford Infants and junior school was opened and in 1901, an embroidery school, for youngsters with learning difficulties, was opened. Two years later in the July of 1903, the Dr Truell Cottage was opened by the Duchess of Somerset, followed shortly by Faith Cottage which was opened by the Countess of Seafield. In the same year Ethel Bolton Cottage was opened by Lady Hope followed by Jessamine and Mignonette Cottages which were opened by a Mrs Ingleby. The last cottage opened that year was the John Sands Cottage opened by Sir Robert Anderson the theologian. Apart from the cottages Queen Victoria House was opened the same year. It was a quarantine house for girls and young children and consisted of three wings; namely Archibald Morton Wing, Wilson Wing and a Babies wing.

1904 brought the building and opening of more cottages. The cottages were named, Francis Reckitt, Sir George Williams, Crosswell, John Howard Anagas, Henry Mountain, Gustasp, and Cannizaro and they were officially opened by HRH Princess Henry of Battenberg nee Princess Beatrice of Great Britain.

The following year was the year that Thomas Barnardo died but not before cottages Joy, Larchfield and McCulloch were opened and the Edmund Hanny Watts Sanatorium was officially opened. That year of 1905 also saw the opening of a dressmaking school and a cookery school.

The Village home at the time of Thomas's death covered sixty acres comprising sixty four cottages housing thirteen hundred girls from the age of two to sixteen years, plus the educational facilities and hospital buildings.

Before his death Thomas laid the foundation stone for the Young Helper's League cottage and in 1906 James Holmes Lucking cottage was officially opened by Lady Brasscy along with the Young Helper's League cottage. The Young Helper's League was a movement set up in

1891 for youngsters to offer help to others in whatever way they could; it later became known as Barnardo's Helper's League.

Dr Barnardo, during his lifetime, longed intensely for a fully equipped hospital in the grounds of the Girl's Village Home. The hospital was eventually built but not until a few years after Barnardo's death. It was opened in 1911, but how it came about is a rather complicated and convoluted story revolving around one James Page.

*

James Page was a destitute child rescued from the streets of the East End of London, where he lived. He survived by stealing what ever he could, wherever he could until he was saved by Dr Barnardo. Barnardo was passing through the East End in his cab when he saw a gang of children trying to rob a drunken man. The cab was halted and Barnardo alighted and addressed the young thieves, some of whom ran away. Others stopped to listen to the great man. A couple of the boys were placed into the cab and taken to Stepney Causeway where they were assessed. One of these boys was James Page.

Page was cared for and nurtured at Barnardo's until he reached the age of seventeen when he expressed a desire to join the Royal Artillery. He enlisted in the artillery and climbed to the rank of sergeant and was sent to South Africa where he took part in the Zulu and Boer wars. He was mentioned in despatches and awarded a Distinguished Service Medal (DSM) for keeping a gun in action after all the other gunners had been shot down by the Boers.

He later married and migrated to Queensland, Australia where, due to his hard work and dedication, he became independent. He stood for and was elected a Member of The House of Representatives for Maranoa. He was returned to this post for fifteen consecutive years and when the Duchess of Cornwall visited Queensland James Page, one time East End street urchin, was among the Reception Committee.

During his time in politics Page held the position of Chief Whip and was described by the then Prime Minister as one of the most faithful and trustworthy colleagues a Head of State could ever have.

It was James Page himself who announced boldly, at a public meeting given in his honour, that he was an ex-Barnardo's boy and that it was the good doctor himself who had rescued him from a life of crime as a street Arab or child of the gutter and that it was the doctor who was responsible for his new start in life which had led to his success.

Page wrote a letter to the representatives of Barnardo's Homes stating that he had no objections about his story being related to other inmates so as to give them hope for the future. He was the archetypal bad boy made good.

When a representative of Barnardo's Homes visited Australia with the object of raising funds for a hospital James Page commended them highly for their efforts and he launched a subscription list among members of the Federal Parliament which he started with a large and generous donation of his own.

The building of the Australasian Hospital was finally realised in 1911 and it was a boon to the children of Barnardo's. It remained open until the late 1960's when the land on which it stood was sold for housing. The name was transferred to two cottages which had been adapted to look after sixteen severely handicapped babies and toddlers and it eventually closed in 1975.

*

CHAPTER FIVE
THE DEATH OF
THOMAS JOHN BARNARDO

By the time he was 50 years old, it had become apparent that Barnardo suffered a heart condition which caused him to slow down his work output. This he did by taking things easier and delegating responsibility, although he was always seen to be in charge.

On the 19th day of September 1905, at his home at St Leonard's Lodge, Surbiton, Thomas Barnardo spent the morning busily collating and reading his correspondence.

In the afternoon he took a short nap to recharge his batteries and in the evening he sat down, with his spouse, to a light dinner. After his light repast he settled into an armchair by the hearth, for a rest. He turned to Syrie and complained that his head felt heavy and asked could he rest his head upon her. A moment later he shuffled off the mortal coil and his soul passed away, hopefully, to a finer place. He was just Sixty years of age. He had died of Angina Pectoris.

*

Angina Pectoris is not a heart attack as such but more of a warning of an attack. It is not a disease but more a symptom and is an indication of atherosclerosis, an accumulation of fatty deposits, (Cholesterol), in the coronary arteries and usually manifesting itself as a tightening in the chest accompanied by severe pain when there is an unusual demand for blood in the heart. This is often accompanied by a feeling of being constricted or suffocated and may also be associated with dizziness and palpitations.

An occasion of Angina Pectoris is usually short and often, the worst is over in minutes, although this was not the case in Barnardo's last moments.

*

It was Thomas' wish that his body be carried to the grave by his friends from the Edinburgh Castle and Stepney Causeway who wished to volunteer for this final service.

The mortal remains of the great man rested, in the coffin, in The Peoples Mission Church at the Edinburgh Castle for five days: from Saturday 23rd until Wednesday 27th September. During these few days thousands of East End people paraded past his body to pay their last respects to a man that they had come to love and admire.

From the Edinburgh Castle and led by the Stepney Boys Band, a huge procession of mourners including boys from all the homes that he had founded and groups of former inmates of the homes plus youngsters from homes in the provinces as well as ninety one boys that were to emigrate to Canada the following day. Perhaps 1500 boys in all followed the cortege.

Directly behind the hearse followed an empty cab which was often used by Thomas John Barnardo, this was led by the doctor's coachman, Peers. Then came all his close family and relatives followed by the President and Vice President of the General Council, distinguished friends, of whom there were many and supporters of his work plus representatives of numerous welfare societies such as the NSPCC etc. Following on was an immense crowd of the general public.

Most businesses, along the funereal route, closed for the day out of respect for this most noble of gentlemen. The blinds of the great majority of residences along the route to Liverpool Street Station had their blinds drawn shut for the same reason. The roadside along the route was lined by mourners four or more deep, some crying openly and bowing their heads in reverence, others sobbing behind their handkerchiefs.

A special train had been arranged to carry the body of Thomas John to Barkingside Station, which had only recently been opened. At

Barkingside the funeral cortege was re-formed and proceeded the quarter of a mile to the Girl's Village Home passing, on its way, long lines of weeping children and adults who had seen fit to honour Barnardo on his final trip.

The service to honour the great man was held in a large marquee inside the Village grounds by the Bishop of Barking, the Reverend H. Newton, the Reverend A.P. McNeill and Canon Fleming. Reverend Newton was the clergyman of the church in Surbiton at which Barnardo attended and the Reverend A.P. McNeill was the Chaplain of the Boys' homes.

Finally, on Wednesday 4th October, seven days after the service, the interment took place in the grounds of the Girl's Village Home, in front of Cairns House, a place that Barnardo had intimated to whilst alive.

A memorial to Dr Barnardo, designed by Sir George Frampton R.A., was unveiled on Friday 19th June 1908, at Barkingside, close to the grave of the beloved Doctor, in front of Cairns House. The whole memorial which is twenty feet in height, was designed and erected free of charge.

After the death of Thomas John Barnardo, William Baker became the Honorary Director of Barnardo's Homes.

CHAPTER SIX
WOODFORD BRIDGE BOYS GARDEN CITY
& LABOUR HOUSE FOR DESTITUTE YOUTHS

During his lifetime and due to the success of The Girl's Village Home, Dr Barnardo wanted to replicate that great achievement by building A Village Home for boys. After his death, Gwynne House at Woodford Bridge in Essex was offered to the Council of Barnardo's Homes. It was a fine old building with plenty of office and accommodation room and was set in thirty nine acres of land.

The offer of the land and the house came with an option to purchase within three years at a cost of £6,000. William Baker, the then Director of Barnardo's and after whom the William Baker Memorial Technical School was named, and the Barnardo's council accepted the offer.

The aim was to build thirty cottages to house 900 boys and incorporate a church, school, sanatorium, isolation hospital and playground. Although the projected numbers were never achieved, The Boys Garden City was officially opened in 1909 by HRH the Duchess of Albany, four years after the death of Thomas John Barnardo.

*

As well as the first Barnardo's home in Stepney Causeway, another very important establishment opened not long after was Labour House, whose full title was the Labour House for Destitute Youths, situated at 622 to 626 Commercial Road London E.1. At the time it was presided over and managed by one Mr. John Appleton. It was a place where boys learned practical skills such as general woodworking and carpentry. Approximately two hundred youths were normally employed there, their ages ranged from seventeen to twenty two years and their main occupations consisted of wood cutting and the construction of packing cases. The manufacture of aerated drinks and temperance drinks of every kind was also carried out at Labour House.

The Labour House for Destitute Youths was run on a strictly commercial basis and the packing case department serviced some of the largest commercial manufacturing companies in London. The aerated waters division supplied many of the big hotels in the metropolis.

The youths at Labour House served a probationary period of nine or ten months, where after, if they had shown that they were capable and not afraid of hard work, they would be offered a placement in Canada, where they had the opportunity to gain for themselves independence and a comfortable home far away from the life of destitution and squalor that blighted their younger lives.

Labour House originally opened in 1882 and was closed in 1909 when the boys were moved to Gwynne House, Woodford Bridge. The home had been brought to fruition by William Baker and was modelled on the original concept of The Girl's Village Home.

The first thirty four boys in residence at The Boy's Garden City came from Labour House and Sheppard House in the East End of London. The Doctor Barnardo Council wished to close some of the older East End Homes, which were becoming cramped, and move the residents to the more comfortable, custom built Boy's Garden City, in the countryside.

The first five houses to open on the new site were: King Edward VII House, Dr Barnardo House, Canon Fleming House, Samuel Gurney Sheppard House and Empire House. Each was different in detail using different coloured brick and differing styles of construction, to give them some individuality.

The next eight houses built were: Angus House, Ackworth House, Christine House, Lucking House, Natal House, Pellew House, Union Jack House and Barnardo's Saturday House.

It had taken over thirty years to build The Girl's Village Home and only three years to get The Boy's Garden City up and running and in 1913 the last three houses were built and opened, they were: Britannia House, New Zealand House and Kempstone House and each house was occupied by thirty four boys.

The boys attended four local schools; they grew their own vegetables and repaired their own boots. Basket weaving was also taught. Each house had its own housemother who was aided by an assistant who supervised the boys as they made their own beds and scrubbed and cleaned; the older boys worked on the land to produce the vegetables used in feeding the home.

In the grounds of the Boy's Garden City, a huge building was erected. The building was named Canada Hall and within the Hall each house would have its own table where the boys would dine. Canada Hall contained the kitchen where all the cooking could be carried out centrally.

In 1921 a new bakery was built and three more houses were erected and opened, these were: McCall House, Corby House and Wakefield House.

Woodford Bridge finally closed its doors as a residential home for boys in September 1977.

*

It was to Woodford Bridge Boys Garden City that my father was sent on the twenty eighth day of August 1930, he was ten years and nine months old. His elder half sister Louisa Maud Juliet was, on the same date, taken in at the Girl's Village Home, she was just thirteen.

My father was the illegitimate son of Nellie Smith and a French speaking Swiss waiter called Auguste Burnier, who was working in London and whom Nellie had taken up with whilst her husband, Ernest, was away fighting for King and Country. Ernest and Nellie divorced in 1921 and Auguste Burnier moved in with Nellie at her address on St Georges Road, Kennington, near the Elephant and Castle, South of the River Thames. Nellie was abused and ill-treated by the Swiss waiter and after giving birth to three children by him, one of whom died in infancy, she eventually had had enough of the beatings and she threw him out. She, apparently, saw or heard nothing more of the Helvetian until 30th March 1944 when his body was pulled from the River Thames, close to Wandsworth Gas Works. The death certificate stated that "he had died of asphyxia due to drowning. He took his own life whilst the balance of his mind was disturbed." Nellie went on to marry again, a man named Benjamin Mills.

The two surviving children of the Swiss waiter were Charles William and my father Auguste Burnier. Louisa was the only legitimate child of Nellie and Ernest Smith. There is no account of Charles being taken in to Barnardo's or of his life in the intervening years, but he eventually ended up in Australia where he joined the Anzac's and was killed on active service in Singapore.

Finding that she could no longer support herself and the children, Nellie made application on behalf of the two boys, who were unwanted and unloved, and who were sent to school in a dirty, ill clad and neglected condition. At one point the mother withdrew the application, hoping to get the boys admitted to the Hanwell Schools, which were schools for orphaned and destitute children that were ran by the local authority, but as the local authorities refused to take them, the application to Barnardo's was renewed.

Admission to Barnardo's was offered to the elder boy, Auguste Burnier and the girl Louisa Maud. Auguste Burnier was a bright, healthy, intelligent boy and showed a desire to be trained as a sailor. Louisa, also, was healthy and of normal intelligence.

Louisa and Auguste, although they were only half kin were very close and my father told me a tale, though not verified, of how he absconded, one day, from the Boy's Garden City at Woodford Bridge, made his way the two miles or so across to the Girl's Village Home at Tanner's Lane, Barkingside and apparently freed his sister. They ran away with very little idea of where they were going but were soon caught and taken back to their respective places of incarceration. As I am sure that that is how they viewed the homes at the time. Similarly to the tales of bullying, as with the tale of absconding I got the feeling that my father only told me what he wanted me to hear.

Boys in the home could partake in many activities and sports and Gus despite being diagnosed as myopic and having to wear spectacles was taught the noble art of pugilism. He apparently enjoyed boxing and when in the ring fought under the name of "Boy Pepper," Pepper being his mother's maiden name. He must have been quite adept at the sport as he never had his nose broken and later upon joining the Royal Air Force he represented them fighting under the same name of "Boy Pepper." He was known as "Boy" by all his relatives throughout his adult life and I, upon visiting my relatives in the South was known fondly as Boy's boy.

When Auguste reached the age of fifteen he was found employment with a Miss Fleming of 143 Park Lane in the West End, as a kitchen boy, at the rate of twelve and sixpence per week (62 1/2p) plus board and lodgings. After a while his mother took him back in because he was earning a wage, it wasn't much but in those days every penny counted. He stayed at his mother's home until he joined the RAF at the outbreak of WWII. This was somewhat surprising considering his early desire to be trained as a sailor. After enlisting, because of his poor eyesight, Gus could only be employed as ground staff. After the cessation of hostilities Gus was sent on a training course for plumbing and gas fitting, which he passed with flying colours and a diploma which enabled him to find gainful employment upon leaving the RAF.

Pictured on the following page are,

Top, Auguste Burnier and his half sister Louisa Maud, upon their induction into Barnardo's

Bottom, Auguste Burnier's official photograph for The Woodford Bridge Boy's Garden City

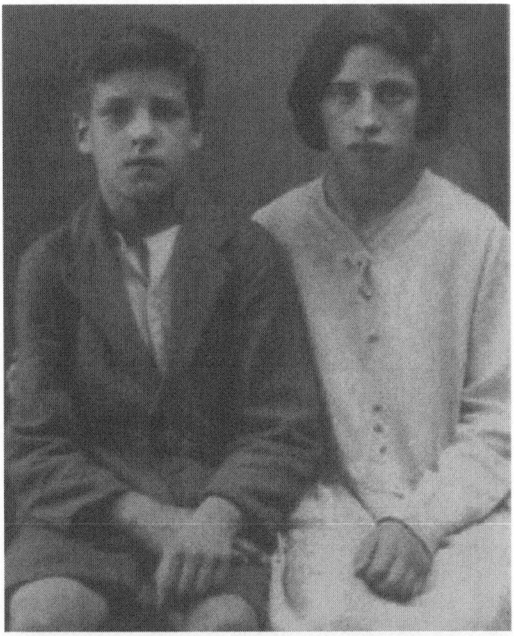

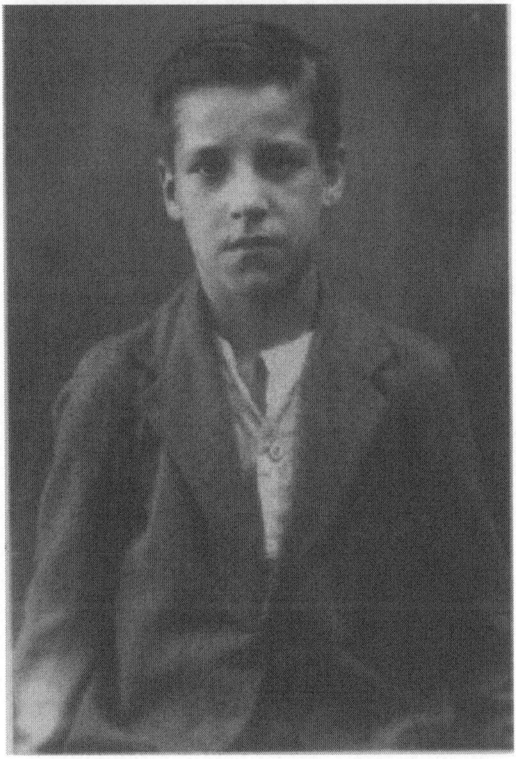

The report on Auguste and Louisa, by a Dr Barnardo's Inspector

LOUISA MAUD JULIET & AUGUSTE BERNIER SMITH

Admitted—28th August, 1930.

LOUISA Age—13 yrs. 1 mo.   Born—12th July, 1917, in St. Thomas Hospital, Westminster.
AUGUSTE   10 yrs. 9 mos.   „   5th Nov. 1919, in Lambeth Hospital.
Mother—Church of England.
If Baptised—Yes, both.
Full Agreements—signed by mother.

Father of Louisa—Ernest Smith, soldier, who divorced mother in 1921, no other particulars.
Father of Auguste—Boy illegitimate (see below)
Mother—Nellie Sarah Smith, known as Mrs. Bernier (35), kitchen-maid, 22/- p.w., health good, character poor, 83, St. Georges Road, Kennington, S.E.

Auguste illegitimate. Application by mother. Investigated by one of our officers.

The mother was married at St. Peter's Church, Streatham, on 25/12/16, to Ernest Smith, a soldier, and Louisa was their only child. During his absence in France the mother met the putative father of Auguste, a Swiss waiter, where the mother was employed as a waitress. Smith obtained a divorce in 1921, and the putative father went to live with the mother at the grandmother's, and she bore him three children, one of whom died in infancy. The man did but little work, and knocked the mother about, and in June, 1929, the grandmother turned him out of the house. The mother said she had not seen him since, and did not wish to have anything more to do with him. Finding she could not support herself and children, she made application on behalf of the two boys, who were unwanted and unloved, and were sent to school in a dirty, ill-clad, neglected condition. At one point the mother withdrew the application, hoping to get the boys admitted to the Hanwell Schools, but as the local Authorities refused to take them, the application to us was renewed.

Admission was offered to the elder boy and the girl, Louisa. Auguste was a bright, healthy, intelligent boy, and wished to be trained as a sailor. Louisa also was healthy and of normal intelligence. The mother was advised to find the putative father and affiliate the boys. The children last resided at 83, St. Georges Road, Kennington, S.E.

Relatives:—

Putative father of Auguste—Auguste Bernier (41), waiter, health good, character poor, whereabouts unknown, Swiss.
Brother (also half-brother)—Charles Wm. Bernier (so registered) (8), with mother.
Grandmother—Sarah J. Pepper (68), w., charwoman, 83 St. Georges Road, Kennington.
Uncles and aunt (mat.)—Reginald V. Pepper (48), labourer, m. 2 children, 15 Cross Street, Chatham; Wallace G. Pepper (46), m. 5 children, Council House, Dagenham (a wounded soldier, at present in Military Hospital, Portsmouth); Louisa Gohriger (40), m. 1 child, in Switzerland.

Report on Auguste's appointment into domestic service

SITUATION BOOK

Name of Boy: Smith, Auguste Bernier   Age: 15yrs. 2months

Date and Place of Birth: Date of Admission:
5th November 1919, Lambeth Hospital   28th August 1930

                                                        Record: Good

Name and Address of Employer: Miss Fleming, Park Lane Court, 143 Park Lane, W.

Date of Engagement: 23rd January 1935

Nature of Employment: Kitchen Boy

Terms of Engagement: 12/6 Board Lodging & Work

Inmate: Boys Garden City

REPORTS

2.2.35	Copy of lad's B.C. sent to lad.
11.2.35	Lad's mother, Mrs. N. Smith, 83 St. George's Road, Southwark, informed he is being given a further trial.
20.2.35	Lad left situation and returned home.
26.3.35	Request from mother for lad's birth certificate. Reply we have not got it. Suggest application be made.
1937	Christmas letter returned. "Not Known".

Auguste Burnier, Aged Fifteen, Dressed and Groomed
Before Taking up His Job as a Kitchen Boy,
a Position Found For Him by The Woodford Bridge, Boy's Garden City

CHAPTER SEVEN
WATTS NAVAL TRAINING SCHOOL

The building in which The Watts Naval Training School was housed dated from 1871 when it was built as a County School for fee paying students. It was built by Mr Edmund Hanny Watts, a local farmer and landowner, as an agricultural school for the training of gentlemen farmers. The school was situated at North Elmham, near Dereham, Norfolk. It was approximately fifteen miles from Norwich and twelve miles from the sea.

When Edmund Hanny Watts unfortunately died, his eldest son, Mr Fenwick S. Watts took on his father's mantle, but because the County School was never a financial success it was donated to Dr Barnardo's homes in 1901 as an establishment to train boys for a life of seamanship. Mr Fenwick S. Watts set about refurbishing the building and installing various fitments at the personal cost of £13,000.

The Naval School officially opened in 1903 by King Edward VII, Prince of Wales, and when it was transferred to Dr Barnardo's, it was one of the most complete institutions of its kind in England.

The Watts Naval Training School accommodated up to three hundred and twenty boys and admission to the school was open to orphan and destitute boys between the ages of eleven and fourteen. They lived a military style life and were issued numbers by which they were identified rather than by their names. Their days were controlled by the bugle and the whistle. Their hair was clipped short in the military style of the day and they were issued with sailors' uniforms.

The captain of the 'ship' at the time was Commander H.C. Martin of the Royal Navy; formerly captain of the training ship Warspite. He was assisted, in his duties, by fifteen staff made up of both men and women.

The regime at Watts seems relatively harsh by today's standards. The cane was used to punish transgressions of the school rules. The boy's best uniform and socks and boots were stowed away in lockers and the youths would go barefoot, whether indoors or outside the building. The only exceptions were for church services and Sunday parade when socks and boots were worn.

The boy's days started at 5.45am and the first hour was spent sweeping, cleaning, scrubbing and polishing, tasks that, on an ocean going ship would have been known as swabbing the decks. After the cleaning etc came breakfast and then assembly. At 9.15am classes would commence and continue through to 4.50pm. As well as the standard lessons such as Maths and English etc the boys would learn seamanship, physical training, gunnery, drill and signals.

Evenings were also a busy time. The boy's would have their evening repast, do their homework. They would then be served supper, after which hundreds of boys would line up for the teeth cleaning ceremony whereby each boy would be issued with a teaspoonful of salt with which to clean their teeth and gargle. They would then shower and turn in. Lights out was 9.00pm. Through the night the boys would take turns at sentry duty.

Life was tough at Watts, but like the modern day services, once the boys had buckled down and made it through the first few weeks, the initial breaking in period, they grew to love their, somewhat, unusual school.

Watts was classed as a Secondary Technical School but would be better described as a Naval Preparatory School. The technical side of the learning leaned heavily towards nautical subjects and also musical tuition for those boys that showed a musical inclination and aptitude and who wished to be enlisted, as bandsmen in the Royal Marines or other military bands. The training given at Watts Naval School enabled the boys to have a good start in their naval careers. Those that wished to carry on with the naval training and continue into the Royal Navy were, after their time at Watts, sent to the HMS Ganges, a boy's Naval training establishment at Shotley, Suffolk.

Not all the boys who attended Watts, however, ended up following a seafaring career. Boys were sent there that would benefit from the type of group education that they received and those that might benefit from the healthy, outdoor routine of the school. For those that changed their minds about a nautical career, there was no compulsion. Other trades such as carpentry were taught and although it might be assumed that a lot of the nautical training may have been in vain, that was not necessarily the case, because besides learning their normal lessons, those instructions of a nautical nature served to broaden the education of the students.

Watts Naval Training School closed its doors in 1949 but during its time many former pupils distinguished themselves in action in both World Wars. It was after the 1914 – 18 war that the Watts School, because of the distinction gained by its former pupils, won praise from the Admiralty itself. It was on the success of Watts that Dr Barnardo's Council, in 1919, opened the Russell-Cotes School for Nautical Seamen in Dorset. Russell-Cotes was about half the size of Watts and was aimed at training boys for the Mercantile Marine as opposed to Watts whose trainees, mainly served in the Royal Navy.

The foundation stone for The Russell-Cotes School was laid by HRH Prince Albert and the school was officially opened in 1922. The money and land for the project, thirty four acres situated three and a half miles from Bournemouth and one mile North-East of Poole, was donated by Sir Merton and Lady Russell-Cotes who were involved in charity work and with the overseeing of the development of the property for Dr Barnardo's.

After the Second World War and because it was peacetime there did not seem to be the same number of boys who wanted to train as seamen so it was deemed sensible to amalgamate both Watts and Russell-Cotes as one school at the site of Russell-Cotes Naval Training School, mainly because this was a more modern structure and more suited to modern times. In 1951 the name of the school was changed to the Parkstone Sea Training School and Parkstone finally closed in 1964.

CHAPTER EIGHT
MEDICAL CARE & THE MILNE FAMILY AT BARNARDO'S

Although the boys and girls in Barnardo's homes were looked after and received adequate health care from the outset, it wasn't until February 1880, when there was an outbreak of Scarlet Fever at the Girl's Village Home that Dr Barnardo searched for help further afield. This help came in the form of Dr Robert Milne.

Dr Milne was born on a farm in Peterculter, Deeside, Aberdeenshire in 1849. He studied at the Aberdeen Grammar School and received his medical education at Marischal College, Aberdeen where he qualified and graduated in 1874.

His intentions, similar to those of Dr Barnardo, were to go to China as a medical missionary. It is supposed that it was in Edinburgh that Milne and Barnardo first met. It was whilst Dr Milne was working as an assistant to Dr Burns Thomson of Edinburgh that he was diagnosed as having tuberculosis of the hip joint. He returned to Aberdeenshire where he was confined to bed for a year. In 1876 he started a practise in Midmar, Aberdeenshire, at the time he was still on crutches. It was while he was running his practise in Midmar that he received the urgent invitation from London to deal with the outbreak of Scarlet Fever.

Dr Milne advocated the use of Eucalyptus oil or carbolic oil in the treatment of Scarlet Fever by way of anointing the throat with these oils during the first few days of the fever. The applications as performed under Dr Milnes instruction, and known as 'The Milne Method' rendered isolation unnecessary.

In the following May Dr Milne became the medical officer to Dr Barnardo's Homes and for nearly forty years he remained as the Chief Medical Officer. He retired at the end of 1919. He died November 8th 1922 of a haemorrhaging ulcer, leaving a widow, five daughters and three sons.

In 1904 he was joined by his eldest son, Dr James Milne (1878-1950), in the position of Medical Officer, firstly at Her Majesty's Hospital, Stepney and then at the John Capel Hanbury Hospital at The Boys Garden City. James held the position of Medical Officer for forty years from 1904 to 1944.

Another of his sons, Surgeon Rear-Admiral Robert Milne (1881-1945) served as the Honorary Consultant Surgeon to Barnardo's.

His daughter Nurse Mary Milne OBE (1892-1972), was a member of the Council from 1952 to 1969 and Vice President from 1969.

Dr (Robert) Ian Milne (1916-1969), son of the younger Robert, was a member of the Council from 1959, Deputy Chairman from 1962 and later the Chairman of the Council.

No family has had closer, medical relationship with Barnardo's Homes than the Milne Family. Five members of the family served Barnardo's over a period of ninety years.

CHAPTER NINE
HINTS OF CONTROVERSY AND CORRUPTION AT BARNARDO'S HOMES

From virtually the first day of opening his first rescue home, Barnardo's was open to controversy and accusations of corruption. Dr Barnardo, himself, was seen to be strong minded and dogmatic; a man that ignored any rules that he considered inconvenient and that hampered, in any way, his work with the orphans and destitute children that he wished to protect.

By 1896 the Doctor had made eighty eight court appearances, mainly on the charge of kidnapping. He admitted, quite freely, that "I have rescued, or abducted, if you wish, children from the custody of parents and guardians who were leading immoral lives; or who, by their conduct, were about to inflict grievous wrong upon the children in their care." Those things he did for reasons that he believed to be right and to protect and give those he was accused of abducting a more normal life.

Another charge laid against the Doctor was that he was not entitled to use that title. As told earlier in these pages, he interrupted his medical studies, but later returned to medical school and passed his examinations in Edinburgh where he was elected a Fellow of the Royal College of Surgeons, Edinburgh 1880. Still, some believed that he was not entitled to use the honorific title of doctor.

There were accusations of maltreatment of children, the faking of photographs, failure to provide proper moral and religious training and the neglecting of simple sanitary precautions. Barnardo hit back at his accusers and critics by calling for arbitration, under a court order in 1877. The arbitrators rejected, unanimously, all the charges against him.

Even the boarding out and emigration programs were open to controversy with accusations that some émigrés to the colonies and indeed, some of those fostered out in Great Britain were treated cruelly in their new homes and that they were used as free or slave labour, incurring beatings, being underfed and at times being locked in darkened rooms and other forms of maltreatment including sexual abuse. These accusations led to the drawing up of a contract to ensure that the émigrés became part of their adopted families and were treated as such.

In 2002 Barnardo's was involved in a lawsuit when it was accused of shipping destitute children from Britain to Canada to become little more than farm servants. The action was launched by Ontario's Supreme Court of Justice and alleges that the charity sent youngsters to Canada while they still had parents living in Britain and that those children were abused and forced to work up to eighteen hours a day, seven days a week and with little food. The action was launched on behalf of an Eighty six year old former Barnardo's boy who was shipped to Canada at the age of fourteen when his single mother could no longer look after him and he was put into the care of Doctor Barnardo's suffering from rickets. It was said that, although Barnardo's intentions seemed praiseworthy to some, it is an indisputable fact that many of the migrant children were cruelly mistreated and that such mistreatment must have been known or at least suspected by some of Barnardo's representatives.

There have been suggestions that the Great Doctor himself could have been none other than Jack the Ripper. Incredible though the suggestions may seem, they were based on the facts that TJ Barnardo was well known in and around the East End of London and in particular the Whitechapel and Bethnal Green areas. He was known to visit doss houses and brothels and to converse with and preach to prostitutes wherever they plied their trade in order to encourage them to turn their offspring over to his care. He was often to be seen out at night, in his coach, seeking out destitute and homeless children, to take into care.

It was proposed that his religious zeal led him to murder the ladies of the night to clear the streets of prostitutes and to prevent them from bearing children. In fact, Barnardo's only connection with the Ripper was that, 'Long' Liz Stride, one of the women to whom he had preached, became the fourth victim of Jack the Ripper days later.

At institutions like Barnardo's Homes, there have always been rumours of bullying by the boys as well as the staff. Corporal punishment was used, in those unenlightened days, to try to curb any transgressions of the rules by the inmates. The cane was often used at the Naval Training Schools such as Watts and Russell-Cotes and later Parkstone. The canings were administered, usually in the gymnasium, over a vaulting horse, by the Petty Officer with three other officers as witnesses to oversee the punishment and make sure that it did not descend into cruelty and abuse.

There was in charge, from 1934 – 1940, at Watts Naval Training School, one Commander "Flogger" Campbell. He returned to the school in 1943 after receiving a war wound. The wound, however, did nothing to slow down his caning arm.

There was a mass absconding in 1946, some think out of devilment rather than anything more serious. When the boys were returned to the school they had to face the wrath of Campbell who held his equivalent to a Court Martial where every absconder was sentenced to twelve strokes of the cane. "Flogger" carried out the punishment, in the basement Gym, over a two hour period with each lad bent over and strapped to a vaulting horse. The cane was brought down on the boy's bare buttocks and it was said that the screams of the beaten boys could be heard in the classrooms above.

After the canings, two of the boys ran away again and when caught by the police one of them revealed the extent of the punishment that they had received. A police doctor was called in to examine the boys and a formal complaint was forwarded to Barnardo's Homes. Campbell retired shortly after.

That incident is the only known case of abuse at Watts, discipline, generally, was strict but fair.

Controversy still exists within the modern Barnardo's, mainly in the advertisements for the charity. On Friday 28th January 2003, a controversial and hard hitting advertising campaign showed a baby with a heroin syringe in its mouth. The advert caused a storm and elicited a number of complaints which led to the offending picture being replaced with one of a bonny, bouncing baby.

Another advertisement for Barnardo's featured the F word numerous times, even though the word was spelt out thus: F**K, it again elicited a number of complaints.

A third advertisement showed a baby with a cockroach emerging from its mouth and yet another showed a baby with a bottle of methylated spirits to its lips. The banner for these adverts was "There are no silver spoons for children born into poverty." All of the above advertisements were banned but more recently another one has been broadcast showing a girl, supposedly a junkie, being repeatedly slapped around the head. The advert depicts an abused teenager failing in her schoolwork and spiralling into heroin addiction, linking the three things, abuse, academic failure and addiction together. An altogether too common occurrence as far as modern day abuse goes.

After seeing all of these advertisements and seeing them in context, I somewhat agree with Barnardo's decisions to show them. It seems that in the modern world the only way, sometimes, to get ones point across, is to use shock tactics and if these shock tactics work…..Well?

CHAPTER TEN
BOARDING OUT AND EMIGRATION FROM BARNARDO'S

Thomas Barnardo's long held belief was that the best way forward for a child to be brought up was in a stable family relationship rather than in institutions. To this end he started to look at the feasibility of a system whereby children would be fostered out to respectable and stable, working class families. After thorough research into what was required and what standards were to be set, his first scheme for boarding out started in 1886/1887 when three hundred boys were sent to good homes, well away from the slums, deprivation and pollution that he believed were the causes of their physical and moral breakdown. He chose, for the schemes, children between the ages of five and nine years of age because it was his belief that institutional life had a more adverse affect on younger children.

Foster parents were paid five shillings per week, per child and were expected to be God-fearing people earning a living, preferably teetotal and have in place clean comfortable accommodation with satisfactory sanitary arrangements. The preference for at least one of the foster parents to be a wage earner was deemed necessary so that the foster payment would not be the sole source of income. Besides the financial and contractual arrangements, Barnardo appointed doctors to visit the foster homes on a random basis to check on and report on the foster children's welfare and the living conditions within the homes.

After his death in 1905 Barnardo's practices and views were seen as remarkably modern with over half the children of Barnardo's homes being boarded out with foster parents.

From the start Thomas John Barnardo believed that the most vulnerable of children deserved the best start in life and that philosophy still stands in the charity today. Barnardo's reputation for training all its boys for a trade meant that many homeless children applied for a place within the care of Barnardo's. Girls who ended up in the care of Barnardo Homes were trained for domestic service and although that hardly applies to modern times, domestic service was considered a worthy option at the time for girls at the end of the nineteenth century and the beginning of the twentieth. The training provided them with skills relevant to the time and enabled them to earn a living and gave them the necessary skills for homemaking.

Barnardo's ran hundreds of homes throughout the United Kingdom from Thomas Barnardo's early philanthropic days until the 1970's. Prior to and during the Second World War a lot of homes were used as evacuation centres including some stately homes which were given over to the welfare of the evacuated Barnardo's children until a few years after the cessation of hostilities when the stately homes and some other large buildings were handed back to their original owners and the children returned to the homes that they had occupied before. Of course, to some, the wartime homes were the only Dr Barnardo's home that they knew and others who were only children at the start of the war had reached working age at its end.

Emigration to the colonies was seen as another way of giving disadvantaged children a fresh start away from the places that blighted their young lives. Barnardo's was by no means the first to use this option for the betterment of the under privileged children. From as early as the seventeenth century when one hundred vagrant children were sent from London to Jamestown, Virginia in North America, to the first English settlement there, it has been going on. The American War of Independence in1783 meant an end to transportation to the American Colonies and so the focus then was on Canada, Australia and New Zealand.

Child emigration was undertaken by charitable and religious organisations. The Children's Friend Society was one of the earliest of those. They sent their first party of child migrants to Australia in 1832. The ragged school movement, in 1844, sent one hundred and fifty children to New South Wales. From 1870 to 1936 the Orphan Homes of Scotland founded by William Quarrier and known as the Quarrier Homes, participated in the British Child Relocation Program which sent more than seven thousand youngsters to Canada. Many of those relocated children were employed as farm labourers on poor pay. The Irish had homes built on the same model and principles known as Smyly Homes based in Dublin.

Founded in 1853, The Children's Aid Society in New York sent orphans further afield from New York by what was known as the "orphan train" to the Mid-West farming states of Kansas, Ohio, Michigan, and Iowa. The idea of sending children to schools to be trained as farm workers was adopted in London by one Annie McPherson a Scottish evangelist. She escorted her first party of one hundred children to the reception centre that she had organised in Belleville, Ontario, Canada. She sent other parties of children to her receiving homes of Marchmont and Galt in Ontario and to Knowlton in Quebec. She also arranged emigration for children from Dr Barnardo's Homes, The Quarrier Homes in Scotland and The Smyly Homes of Dublin as well as from her own Home of Industry in London.

The Salvation Army founded by William Booth was also involved in migration to Canada in the late nineteenth century. They helped adults who wished to emigrate but mainly it was children. After WWI they sent migrants to Australia especially farm boys who were trained at a special training camp at Riverview, Brisbane, which was owned and ran by the Salvation Army. Fegan's Homes also known as Fegan's Child and Family Care was founded by James Fegan. His first home was founded in Deptford in1872 and Fegan was responsible for sending over three thousand boys to his homes in Brandon, Manitoba and Toronto between 1884 and 1938. There were other organisations involved with child migration such as Middlemore Homes founded by John T Middlemore in Birmingham which sent children to Ontario in1873 and later in 1893 to Nova Scotia and between 1925 and 1955 to Australia in association with Fairbridge Farm Schools. The first farm school of the Child Emigration

Society of Oxford was established by Kingsley Fairbridge at Pinjarra near Perth, Australia in 1912 and as the Fairbridge Society became leaders of the Farm School Movement and were instrumental in the emigration of over three thousand five hundred children to Australia, The Children's Society sent out approximately four thousand children to Australia, Canada and Southern Rhodesia, and various catholic societies were involved with the migration of children. The Douglas Industrial Home on the Isle of Man sent children along with those from the Quarrier Homes, via Annie McPherson, to Ontario.

Apparently some one hundred and thirty thousand destitute and orphaned children were shipped off to various parts of the British Empire over a period of three hundred and fifty years. Those organisations genuinely believed that they were providing the émigrés with a new start in life but some of the so called respectable families to whom they were fostered viewed their new charges as nothing more than cheap labour and during Barnardo's involvement tales of abuse were soon brought to the attention of the directors. This led to the drawing up of a contract which all prospective foster parents had to sign. The contract stated:-

Any foster child had to be brought up as one of the family and be cared for and nurtured as one of their own. The child had to be well fed, clothed and educated and taught to be truthful, obedient and versed in the ways of personal hygiene and industry. Attendance at church or chapel was a stated promise. Foster parents had to notify and report to the directors any illness suffered by the child and ensure the attendance of a medical doctor. All correspondence was to be read and censored and foster parents were not allowed to enter into correspondence with any person claiming a relationship with the child.

Under the fostering system, many children, from various Barnardo establishments, emigrated to a new and better life in Canada, South Africa, Australia and other countries.

The migration of children to the British Colonies was also seen as a way of populating those far away countries with British stock. It is said, that Dr Barnardo was the most influential person involved in that traffic in the latter part of the nineteenth century and his first party, consisting of fifty boys was sent to Canada in 1882; the migration of girls started a year later. Dr Barnardo had become a famous and much liked philanthropist by this time and with his eloquence and powers of persuasion he presented child migration as a necessary policy to remove children from their early, poverty ridden roots. He was able to convince the governments of the colonies, such as Canada, that it was the right thing to do for the children. Reception homes were established and from those establishments the children were placed into foster care. Those of school age remained in the homes until their education was complete, after which they were fostered out. Between 1882 and 1939 Barnardo's Homes sent over thirty thousand children to Canada. Although there were certainly cases of abuse, not all the children suffered and most actually profited from a better life in a warmer climate with endless opportunities.

CHAPTER ELEVEN
BARNARDO'S TODAY

Barnardo's today still has its Head Office at Tanners Lane, Barkingside, Ilford, Essex, close to the Girl's Village Home as was. Its administration is run through four National Offices, one each in England, Northern Ireland, Scotland and Wales, it has six Regional Offices in England, these being in the East and South East of London, the Midlands, the South West, and in the North West, the North East and Yorkshire.

Eleven of the remaining cottages at the Girl's Village have been sold and turned into flats for retired people while others are used as offices and others have been preserved to stand as a reminder of the good work done in the fledgling days of Barnardo's. The Barkingside Church built in 1894 still remains and is used for staff services and for weddings, funerals etc. Queen Victoria House is now the local registry office. There is also a memorial garden to HRH Diana Princess of Wales (1961-1997) who was the President of Barnardo's from 1984 to 1996

There are no longer any Barnardo's orphanages. Neither are there any residential homes in the old, accepted sense. What was once Dr Barnardo's Homes became Dr Barnardo's and is now known solely as Barnardo's and it is a charity that deals with modern children's needs in a way that is appropriate to today. The charity today still believes, as did Dr Barnardo, that a child's best welfare lies within a family environment and to this end sees long term fostering as the best solution to the problem of child poverty.

Poverty as described by Professor Peter Townsend of The Child Poverty Action Group is as follows: - *Individuals, families and groups can be said to be in poverty when they lack the resources to obtain the types of diet, participate in activities and have the living conditions and amenities which are customary or at least widely encouraged and approved, in the societies in which they belong.*

The Oxford English Dictionary defines it Thus:-*The condition of or quality of being poor, the condition of having little or no wealth or material possessions; indigence; destitution; want; deficiency; lack; scantiness; dearth; scarcity; smallness of amount; deficiency in the proper or desired quality; inferiority; paltriness; meanness.*

Poor as defined by the OED; is as follows: *Having few, or no, material possessions; wanting means to procure the comforts or necessaries of life; needy, indulgent, destitute; spec, (in legal use) so destitute as to be dependent upon gifts or allowances of subsistence. In common use expressing various degrees, from absolute want to straitened circumstances.*

None of these definitions seems, adequately, to portray the actual physical state of abject poverty or convey the image of those that suffer such poverty.

Modern society has introduced a number of initiatives to try to end child poverty and poverty in general. Not least of these is the introduction of the minimum wage which has gone a long way to minimising income poverty. The Welfare State or Social Security has helped in many ways since its introduction in 1948 although, as can be seen by various newspaper reports, it is open to wide abuse.

Barnardo's in its modern guise is a far cry from the ragged schools and orphanages set up in the late 19th and early 20th centuries but its beliefs are still that every child deserves the best possible start in life whether they have been sexually, physically or mentally abused. The aim of the charity is to give all children the chance to fulfil their potential no matter if they are homeless, working as prostitutes or destitute. So Barnardo's vision for children today is much the same as the one Thomas John Barnardo had when he first arrived in the East End of London in 1866; that is, that all children, despite their colour, creed, sex or religion should be free from abuse, discrimination and poverty, whether the cause is substance abuse, mental health, crime, domestic violence or any other cause, Barnardo's believes that it can help.

Funds are essential to the running of Barnardo's and the charity's shops are a great and significant source of income. There are close to three hundred and fifty Barnardo's Charity Shops in the United Kingdom which accept all manner of goods from the general public to be sold on to other members of the public so as to raise the ever needed cash to enable the charity to do its good works.

Fund raising is a necessity for all charities and to this end Barnardo's holds charity auctions and various other fund raising events such as sponsored marathons and fun runs whereby contestants are sponsored to raise money for Barnardo's. There are National and International fund raising events backed by the athlete Daley Thompson. Funds are also raised by on-line donations, via direct debit, through the pay bill and even by the bequeathing of a lump sum in a will.

The Charity employs some six thousand staff across the UK and has branches in Australia which were initiated through the early migration scheme. In New Zealand they run twenty early learning centres. Barnardo's is Ireland's leading, independent children's Charity and has worked in Ireland since 1962.

Although, in the modern world, we still, sadly, have a massive problem with poverty, especially child poverty, it is of a different type and has different causes to that of the Victorian era. There is estimated to be close to four million children living in poverty in the United Kingdom, approximately a third of all children living here it is the worst child poverty rate in Europe. The UK also has the highest infant and child mortality rate and the highest instance of teenage pregnancies. Today, with the welfare state and social security, there is free health care and there is really no need for children to be poorly clothed and poorly shod as were their Victorian counterparts. Basic clothing and footwear should be within the reach of everybody and can be bought very cheaply at the supermarkets and the big clothing outlets. Because of misguided priorities within some of the poorly educated, working class families, booze and cigarettes seem to come before child welfare and those social payments are spent on things other than what they should be spent on. Due to modern sanitation and free public conveniences, there is no need for the modern waifs and strays to be unwashed and unclean. There are also public baths, although these are in decline. Ultimately though, some children and families slip through the net.

Victorian, destitute children became parentless because, either, their parents had died due to the numerous outbreaks of cholera and other illnesses or because they had, literally, been thrown out of house and home because they had fell pregnant or because their parents could not afford to support them. A lot of the homeless youngsters of today are without homes because they have run away from home to escape parental abuse. Children become homeless for all sorts of reasons and although parental abuse is not the sole reason for homelessness it is certainly a contributing factor. There have been reported cases whereby young parents of low intelligence, have brought children in to the world but lack the wherewithal to look after them. Some children have died at the hands of their guardians and some when a little older run away to escape the abuse only to fall into the hands of pimps and other exploiters and abusers of youth. As in Oscar Wilde's day, there are today, rent boys and young girls who will go to the highest bidder. Sadly a lot of these children have not yet reached the age of consent.

There are some similarities between the Victorian era of child poverty and that of today. Drink and drugs have been the bane of both societies due to the ease that both can and could be obtained. The poor cannot afford to feed their habits and so they steal, rob and mug to get the funds for their next fix. Opium in Victorian times could be legally bought on demand and laudanum, a tincture of opium prepared in alcohol, was widely used for medicinal purposes but often fell into the wrong hands. Ale houses and gin palaces, where children were allowed inside, proliferated. Today alcohol is sold so cheaply and can be easily obtained, even by minors, that it has become one of the main causes of family breakdown. Child prostitution of both sexes, brought about by poverty still exists today as it did before and this brings forward questions of sexual health. Sexually transferred diseases have always been a problem; in Br Barnardo's days it was the well known types such as Gonorrhoea and syphilis. These are still a problem today but with the discovery, by Alexander Fleming (1881-1955), of Penicillin which he discovered by accident, venereal diseases can be easily treated, once diagnosed.

*

Alexander Fleming was born in Ayrshire, Scotland, the son of a farmer. He moved to London at age thirteen where he later studied as a doctor and upon qualifying he began research at St Mary's Hospital Medical School. During World War One he served in the Army Medical Corps and at the end of the war he returned to St Mary's. It was in 1928, whilst studying influenza, that he noticed a mould had developed, accidentally, on a set of Petri dishes being used to grow the Staphylococci germ. He noticed that the mould had created a circular, bacteria free area around itself. He studied the culture more and named it Penicillin. It was, however, two other scientists, an Australian named Howard Florey and Ernst Chain, a refugee from Nazi Germany, who finally isolated the drug and enabled it to be produced commercially. In 1945 Fleming, Florey and Chain shared the Nobel Prize.

*

In modern times a new scourge has affected the sexual well being of a number of children and adults; this is HIV/AIDS, which has grown to become a real cause for concern and is said to have reached epidemic proportions. Research goes on and a cure is being sought but seems a long way off.

Barnardo's in its modern guise runs many and diverse projects and many of these projects are ones that work with Black and Minority Ethnic Communities in order to develop positive relationships and partnerships with and within these minority groups. Around the country, there are several projects working in areas populated by large numbers of people of diverse ethnic backgrounds.

Sickle Cell Anaemia is a disease that affects black people more than white and this is just one area where a project is run by Barnardo's. Other projects include working with black children and other minorities that have been excluded from mainstream education. Yet more projects are of the same type as affect others besides ethnic minorities such as domestic violence, the provision of play centres and crèches for the very young, help for the disabled, special fostering services and parental support groups. Child poverty is still the main concern of Barnardo's and they are working with over one hundred and fifteen thousand children, young people and their families by way of four hundred vital projects across the UK, including counselling, fostering and adoption services, vocational training and disability inclusion groups, Barnardo's aim is to reduce the impact of poverty on children, young people and families through social, economic and community action.

Coming from a poverty stricken background seriously affects a child's educational development; those from poorer homes develop slower than those from richer homes.

Like other charities such as Child Line, Save The children, The Child Poverty Action Group and The N.S.P.C.C; (The National Society for the Protection of Cruelty to Children), Barnardo's seeks to rescue and help these much abused children. It believes that no matter what the problem, be it sexual abuse, parental abuse or any other kind of abuse perpetrated on the young, Barnardo's believes that it can bring out the best in every child.

Printed in Great Britain
by Amazon